DAILY AFFIRMATIONS

FOR THE

GAME OF LIFE

Sound Wisdom Books
by
Florence Scovel Shinn

The Game of Life and How to Play It

90 Daily Decrees and Affirmations for Prosperity

Your Word is Your Wand

The Secret Door to Success

DAILY AFFIRMATIONS FOR THE GAME OF LIFE

A FLORENCE SCOVEL SHINN

Inspirational Quote

Journal

Published and Distributed by

SOUND WISDOM
PO Box 310
Shippensburg, PA 17257-0310

717-530-2122

info@soundwisdom.com

www.soundwisdom.com

This book is a historical artifact. Sound Wisdom has reprinted this work to preserve and share the best wisdom handed down from great men and women in history. Not all of the ideas and beliefs held by these authors remain acceptable in our present time, and Sound Wisdom does not condone or endorse every belief shared within this book. We encourage readers to glean the best timeless wisdom from these pages, while exercising grace toward our ancestors' flaws and forgiveness toward the mistakes of the past.

ISBN 13 TP: 978-1-64095-696-4

For Worldwide Distribution, Printed in the USA

1 2 3 4 5 6 / 28 27 26 25

Foreword

With this book, you can start each morning reading a quote or affirmation written with the timeless wisdom of Florence Scovel Shinn and writing your thoughts in this journal.

Daily Affirmations for The Game of Life: A Florence Scovel Shinn Inspirational Quote Journal offers 160 inspiring affirmations and life lessons to guide you on a journey of faith, abundance, and success.

Each page features a profound quote from Florence Scovel Shinn, paired with space for your personal reflections, affirmations, and intentions.

Whether you're seeking spiritual growth, enhanced motivation, or a deeper connection with your inner self, this journal is your perfect companion.

Why you'll love this journal:

- *Timeless Wisdom:* Draw inspiration from Florence Scovel Shinn's transformative teachings on faith, abundance, and life purpose.
- *Daily Motivation:* Reflect on quotes designed to inspire positive action and personal growth every day.
- *Beautiful Design:* Perfect for gifting to loved ones or using as your personal guide to success and mindfulness.

Start your journey toward a life filled with abundance, joy, and purpose. Allow Florence Scovel Shinn's words to inspire and empower you daily.

Sound Wisdom Publishers

The Word's Power

God's powerful word will be accomplished in my life.

I will study and stand firm on God's Word.

The Power of Your Words

I declare that all my needs are met, in Jesus's name.

I affirm that my bank accounts are overflowing with deposits.

Divine Idea Flash

I will let the divine idea flash into my conscious mind.

Then I will be working according to His divine design.

Truth Sets You Free

I decree that there is no truth in lack or limitation—I stand on God's truth of plenty.

I affirm my dominion over every fog and give thanks for the Son!

An Open Door

I decree that God is my supply and
every day is a good day.

I affirm that I have fearless faith that wins!

Endless Opportunities

I decree that is rightfully mine is
given to me under grace.

I affirm that the Christ in me is risen.

No Lost Opportunities

The tide of destiny has turned and everything comes my way. I banish the past and now live in the wonderful now, where happy surprises come to me each day. There are no lost opportunities.

Supply Is Released

I decree that I'm awake to my good and gather in the harvest of endless opportunities.

I affirm that I am harmonious, poised, and magnetic.

Perfect Faith

I decree that there are no lost opportunities in the Kingdom. As one door shuts, another door opens. There is nothing to fear, for there is no power to hurt.

I affirm walking up to the lion on my pathway and finding an angel in armor and victory in the name of Jesus Christ.

No Happiness in Fear

I believe happiness is earned through perfect control of the emotional nature.

There can be no happiness where there is fear, apprehension, or dread.

With perfect faith in God comes a feeling of security and happiness.

Resentment Be Gone

I decree that I am in perfect harmony. I stand aside and let God make easy and successful my way.

I affirm that new fields of divine activity now open for me. Unexpected doors fly open for me.

Jealousy Kills

Only forgiveness and goodwill can cure you.

When you become harmonious and forgiving, splendid health will return.

Unless...

Unless marriage is built upon the rock
of oneness, it cannot stand.

Two souls with but a single thought,
two hearts that beat as one.

His Gifts

I decree that giving precedes receiving and my gifts to others precede God's gifts to me. Every person is a golden link in the chain of my good.

I affirm that my poise is built upon a rock. I see clearly and act quickly. God cannot fail, so I cannot fail.

With Love

I decree that what God has done for others, He can do for me and more. I am as necessary to God as He is to me, for I am the channel to bring his plan to pass.

I affirm that I will not limit God by seeing limitation in myself. With God and myself, all things are possible.

A Corrupted Picture

Whatever you dislike or hate will surely come upon you; for when we hate, we make a vivid yet corrupted picture in the subconscious mind and it objectifies.

The Warrior Within

I decree that the warrior within me has already won.

I affirm that God's Kingdom is within me and
that His will be done in me and my affairs.

Acquitted or Condemned

Many people have unhappy experiences repeated in their lives. Use your words to neutralize your troubles instead of multiply them. Do not voice your sorrows and they will fade from your life—for by your words, you are justified.

Stepping Stone

I decree that I make friends with hindrances and every obstacle becomes a stepping stone.

I affirm that everything in the universe, visible and invisible, is working to bring me to my own.

Faith Unfurled

I decree thanks that the walls of Jericho fall down and all lack, limitation and failure are wiped out of my consciousness in the name of Jesus Christ.

I affirm that I am now on the royal road of success, happiness, and abundance. All the traffic goes my way.

Not Weary

I decree that I will not weary of well-doing for others, for when I least expect it, I shall reap.

I affirm that Jehovah goes before me and the battle is won. All enemy thoughts are wiped out.

Victorious

I decree that I'm victorious in the name of Jesus Christ.

I affirm that there are no obstacles in divine mind.
Therefore, there is nothing to obstruct my good.

Divine Enthusiasm

Through the spoken word, the divine design may be released to fulfill your destiny. I now see clearly the perfect plan of my life. With divine design in your spirit, your supply of everything you need is endless and immediate. Divine enthusiasm fires you and you will now fulfill your destiny.

Unexpected Wonders

I decree that all obstacles now vanish from my pathway.

I affirm that doors fly open, gates are lifted and I enter the kingdom of fulfillment under grace.

You Reap What You Sow

I decree rhythm, harmony and balance are now established in my mind, body and affairs.

I affirm that new fields of divine activity now open for me and these fields are white with the harvest.

Don't Be Misled

Jesus Christ taught that life is a great game of giving and receiving: whatever we sow we reap. And whatever we send out in word or deed will return just the same to us. What we give, we receive. If we give hate, we will receive hate. If we give love, we will receive love.

Imaginations

What you imagine will sooner or later externalize in your day-to-day experiences. Train yourself to imagine only good things, every righteous desire of your heart: health, wealth, love, friends, perfect self expression, your highest ideals—and sooner or later, you meet your own creations in your outer world.

God's Plan

I decree that my will is powerless to interfere with God's will. God's will is now done in my mind, body, and affairs.

I affirm that God's plan for me is permanent and cannot be budged.

Departments of the Mind

I decree that am true to my heavenly vision.

I affirm that the divine plan of my life now takes shape in definite concrete experiences leading to my heart's desire.

The Subconscious Mind

The conscious mind has been called our mortal or carnal mind. It is the human mind and sees life as it appears to be. It sees death, disaster, sickness, poverty, and limitation of every kind, and it impresses the subconscious. Whatever you feel deeply or imagine clearly is impressed upon the subconscious mind and carried out in minutest detail.

The Supersubconscious Mind

The superconscious mind is the God-mind within each human and is the realm of perfect ideas. There is a place that you are to fill and no one else can fill, something you are to do which no one else can do. In reality, it is your true destiny, or destination, flashed to us from the Infinite Intelligence, who is within you.

Irresistible Power

I decree that I now draw from the universal substance with irresistible power and determination that which is mine by divine right.

I affirm that I will not resist this situation.

Idle-Word Disasters

I confirm that God's divine idea for my good will now come to pass.

I affirm that my good now flows to me in a steady, unbroken, ever-increasing stream of success, happiness, and abundance.

From Lack to Plenty

I decree that the decks are now cleared for divine action and my own comes to me under grace.

I affirm letting go of worn out conditions and worn out things.

Make the First Move

I declare that I have fearless faith that
produces God's will and my heart's desire.

I affirm seeing clearly the blessing
God has given me this day.

No Fear

Nothing stands between you and your highest ideals and every desire of your heart—except doubt and fear. When you can wish without worrying, every desire will be instantly fulfilled. Fear must be erased from the consciousness. It is your only enemy: fear of lack, fear of failure, fear of sickness, fear of loss, and a feeling of insecurity on some plane.

Unexpected Wonders

I decree that all obstacles now vanish from my pathway.

I affirm that doors fly open, gates are lifted and I enter the kingdom of fulfillment under grace.

Substitute Faith for Fear

I decree that my seeming impossible
good now comes to pass.

I affirm that the unexpected now happens.

Obliterate Evil

The object of life is to see clearly good and to obliterate all mental pictures of evil. This must be done by impressing the subconscious mind with a realization of good. Have a firm conviction that only good can come into your life and, therefore, only good can manifest.

Ever-Present Listener

We have ever a silent listener at our side—our subconscious mind. Every thought, every word is impressed upon it and carried out in amazing detail. Speak these words aloud with power and conviction: "I now smash and demolish, by my spoken word, every untrue record in my subconscious mind. They shall return to the dust-heap of their native nothingness, for they came from my own vain imaginings. I now make my perfect records through the Christ within, the records of health, wealth, love and perfect self-expression."

Prepare for Success

I decree now to draw from the abundance of the spheres my immediate and endless supply.

I affirm that all channels are free. All doors are open.

Prepare for Failure

If you ask for success and prepare for failure, you will get the situation you are prepared for.

We must prepare for what we have asked for when there isn't the slightest sign of it in sight.

The Goldmine Within

I decree that I now release the goldmine within me.

I affirm that I'm linked with an endless
golden stream of prosperity, which comes
to me under grace in perfect ways.

Undisturbed by Appearances

The one who knows Spiritual Law is undisturbed by appearance and rejoices while yet in captivity. That is, you need to hold to your vision and give thanks that the end is accomplished. Every good and perfect gift is already awaiting recognition. You can only receive what you see receiving.

Goodness and Mercy

I decree and affirm that goodness and mercy shall follow me all the days of my life and I shall dwell in the house of a abundance forever.

Hold the Vision

You must ever hold the vision of your journey's end and demand the manifestation of what you have already received. It may be perfect health, love, supply, self-expression, home, or friends. They are all finished and perfect ideas registered in God's divine mind, your own superconscious mind.

Two Agree

I decree that my God is the God of plenty and I now receive all that I desire or require and more.

I affirm that all that is mine by divine right is now released and reaches me in great avalanches of abundance under grace in miraculous ways.

Put Away Graven Images

The horseshoe or rabbit's foot contains no power. If you have been trusting in lucky monkeys instead of God, put them away and call on the law of forgiveness, for God will forgive and neutralize your mistakes. Recognize that the only power is God's power who gives to you abundantly.

A Calm Sea

I decree that my supply is endless, inexhaustible and immediate and comes to me under grace in perfect ways.

I affirm that all channels are free and open for my immediate and endless, divinely designed supply. My ships come on a calm sea.

God, The Power

I decree under direct inspiration, wisely and fearlessly, knowing all my success is endless and immediate and solely comes from God.

I affirm that I am fearless in letting idols go, knowing God is my immediate and endless supply.

Superstitions

I decree that I will not follow the desires of my sinful nature.

I affirm that I will not be held captive by superstitions.

Ladders

A friend would not walk under a ladder. I said, "If you are afraid, you are giving in to a belief in two powers, good and evil, instead of one. As God is absolute, there can be no opposing power unless you make the false of evil for yourself. To show you believe in only one Power, God, and that there is no power or reality in evil, walk under the next ladder you see." If you are willing to do something you are afraid to do, you will be set free.

Hatred Versus Love

I decree that anger, resentment, ill will, jealousy and revenge rob people of their happiness and bring sickness, failure and poverty in their wake.

I affirm that resentment has ruined more homes than drink and killed more people than war.

Invisible Strings

Invisible forces are ever-working for those who are always pulling the strings themselves, though they don't know it. Owing to the vibratory power of words, whatever you voice, you begin to attract. People who continually speak of disease invariably attract it. After you know the truth, you cannot be too careful of your words.

Curses

I decree that I'm now deluged with the happiness that was planned for me in the beginning.

I affirm that my barns are full, my cup flows over with joy. My endless good now comes to me in endless ways.

Heal, Bless, Prosper

Words are best used for three purposes: to heal, bless, or prosper. To aid someone to success, you aid yourself to success. The body may be renewed and transformed through the spoken word and clear vision. All disease has a mental component, and to heal the body, first heal your soul. The soul is the subconscious mind and must be saved from wrong thinking.

All Your Heart, Soul, Mind

I decree to having a wonderful joy in a wonderful way, and my wonderful joy has come to stay.

I affirm that happy surprises come to me each day as I ask for love for all.

Love One Another

It is safe to say that all sickness and unhappiness come from the violation of the law of love. Jesus's commandment is that we love one another as He loves us. In asking for love and goodwill, you fulfill the law. I believe that every disease is caused by a mind not at ease.

Mental Inharmony

Any inharmony on the external indicates there is mental inharmony. As the within, so the without. Your only enemies are within. Personality is one of the last enemies to be overcome It was and is Christ's message, peace on earth, goodwill toward all. Your work is to send out goodwill and blessings to everyone, and the marvelous thing is that when you bless someone, that person has no power to harm you.

Live in Harmony

I decree to look with wonder at what is before me.

I affirm to walk boldly up to the lion on my pathway and find it is a friendly puppy.

Rock Solid Harmony

I decree that I am harmonious, happy, radiant, detached from the tyranny of fear.

I affirm that my happiness is built upon a rock. It is mine now and for all eternity.

Your Protected Interests

Goodwill produces a great aura of protection about the one who sends it, and no weapon that is formed against that person shall prosper. In other words, love and goodwill destroy the enemies with yourself; therefore, you have no enemies on the external or the internal. There is peace on earth for those who send goodwill to others.

Vain Imagination

Evil has come from human vain imagination, or a belief in two powers: good and evil. Evil is a false law humans have made for themselves through our soul sleep. Soul sleep means that the human soul has been hypnotized by the race belief of sin, sickness, death, etc., which is carnal or mortal thought, and affairs have out-pictured the illusions.

My Good

I decree that my good now flows to me in a steady, unbroken, ever-increasing stream of happiness.

I affirm that my happiness is God's affair. Therefore, no one can interfere.

Picture Perfect

I decree that God's ideas for me are
perfect and permanent.

I affirm that my heart's desire is a perfect idea in divine mind, incorruptible and indestructible, and now comes to pass under grace.

Right Thinking

The person centered and established in right thinking, the person who sends out only goodwill to others, and the person who is without fear cannot be touched or influenced by the negative thoughts of others. In fact, you can receive only good thoughts, as you send forth only good thoughts.

One Power, God

I decree that as I am one with God, I am now one with my heart's desire.

I affirm my thanks for my permanent happiness, my permanent health, my permanent wealth, my permanent love.

First Feel

To demonstrate your supply, you must first feel that you have received. A feeling of opulence must precede its manifestation.

Bless Your Enemy

I decree that I am one with God, the undivided One, I am one with my undivided love and undivided happiness.

I affirm that the light of Christ within now wipes out all my fear, doubt, anger and resentment.

Transmuted Arrows

Bless your enemy, and you rob him of his ammunition—arrows will be transmuted into blessings. This law is true of nations as well as individuals. Bless a nation, send love and goodwill to every inhabitant, and it is robbed of its power to harm.

Faults

I decree that God's love pours through me
an irresistible, magnetic current.

I affirm that I see only perfection
and draw to me my own.

Life Is a Mirror

We are often cured of our faults
by seeing them in others.

Life is a mirror, and we find only ourselves
reflected in our associates.

Don't Live in the Past

I decree divine love through me now
dissolves all seeming obstacles and makes
clear, easy and successful my way.

I affirm living in the now—accepting
all the future has for me.

Live Fully

Living in the past is a failure method and a violation of Spiritual Law. The robbers of time are the past and the future. Bless the past and forget it if it keeps you in bondage—and bless the future knowing it has in store for you endless joys. Live fully in the now.

Live Suspended

Live suspended in the moment. Look well, therefore, to this day. Such is the salutation of the dawn. Be spiritually alert, ever-waiting your leads, taking advantage of every opportunity.

Completion Day

I decree that my apparent enemy becomes my friend, a golden link in the chain of my good.

I affirm that I'm at peace with myself and with the world.

Wonders and Miracles

It is most necessary to begin the day with right words. Make an affirmation immediately upon waking. For example, "Thy will be done this day. Today is a day of completion. I give thanks for this perfect day. Miracle shall follow miracle, and wonders shall never cease." Make this a habit, and you will see wonders and miracles come into your life.

Wonder-Full

You should never use an affirmation unless it is absolutely satisfying and convincing to your own consciousness, and often, an affirmation is changed to suit different people. For example, the following has brought success to many: "I have a wonderful work in a wonderful way. I give wonderful service for wonderful pay."

More Than Enough

It is your divine right to have plenty, more than enough. This is God's idea, and when you break down the barriers of lack in your own consciousness, the golden age will be yours and every righteous desire of your heart fulfilled.

Boomerangs

I decree that I am free from mistakes
and the consequences of mistakes.

I affirm that I'm under grace and not under karmic law.

The More You Know

Life is a game of boomerangs. Your thoughts, deeds, and words return to sooner or later with astounding accuracy. This is the law of reaping what you sow. The more you know, the more you are responsible. Someone with a knowledge of Spiritual Law but does not practice it, suffers greatly in consequence.

The Lord, The Law

I decree that though my mistakes be as scarlet,
I shall be washed whiter than snow.

I affirm that what didn't happen in the
Kingdom never happened anywhere.

Perfect Idea

The law takes vengeance, not God. God sees humankind perfect, created in His own image, imagination, and given power and dominion. This is the perfect idea of a human, registered in God's divine mind, awaiting our recognition, for we can only be what we see ourselves to be and only attain what we see ourselves attaining.

First See

You first see your failure or success, your joy or sorrow before it swings into visibility from the scenes set in your own imagination.

You Shall Not Covet

I decree that no good thing will be withheld from whoever walks uprightly.

I affirm that there is no power in evil. It is nothing, therefore can only come to nothing.

Obedience

Obedience precedes authority, and the law obeys you when you obey the law. The law of electricity must be obeyed before it becomes your servant. When handled ignorantly, it becomes your deadly foe, so with the laws of mind.

Divine Right

Desire is a tremendous force and must be directed in the right channels, or chaos ensues.

In demonstrating, the most important step is the first step, to ask aright. We should always demand only what is ours by divine right. Anything forced into manifestation through personal will is always ill-got and has ever-bad success.

Stand Still

I decree that fear and impatience demagnetize. Poise magnetizes.

I affirm that I will drown the reasoning mind with my affirmation.

Relinquishment

As a believer you will always get what you desire when you relinquish all personal will, thereby enabling Infinite Intelligence to work through you. This is the "Stand still and see the salvation of the Lord" law. Yet, learning to stand still seems so difficult for humans.

The Law of Forgiveness

I decree that I forgive everyone
and everyone forgives me.

I affirm and call on the law of forgiveness.

Redemption Foundation

Christianity is founded upon the law of forgiveness. Christ has redeemed you from the curse of karmic law, and Christ within you is your Redeemer and salvation from all inharmonious conditions. Knowledge of the law gives you power to rub out mistakes.

Order Versus Disorder

I decree that there is always a way out of every solution.

I affirm that under grace, everyone
is free to do the will of God.

A Burnt Match

If you wish to be rich, you much be orderly. All with great wealth are orderly, and order is Heaven's first law. You will never become rich with a burnt match in the pincushion.

Wise Investments

I decree that sureism is stronger than optimism.

I affirm that divine ideas never conflict.

Leadings

If you ignore leadings to spend or to give, the same amount of money will go in an uninteresting or unhappy way.

According to Your Faith

I decree that it is dangerous to stop
in the middle of a hunch.

I affirm that the Holy Spirit is never too late.

Inexhaustible Supply

Your supply is inexhaustible and unfailing when fully trusted, but faith or trust must precede the demonstration. Jesus says, *"According to your faith be it unto you"* (Matthew 9:29). Faith is the substance of things hoped for and the evidence of things not seen, for faith holds the vision steady, and the adverse pictures are dissolved and dissipated, and in due season, you shall reap, if you faint not (see Hebrews 11:1; Galatians 6:9).

Hope Chest

I decree that hope looks forward.

I affirm that faith knows it has already received and acts accordingly.

Under Grace

I decree that every plan my Father in Heaven has not planned is dissolved and obliterated and the divine design of my life now comes to pass.

I affirm that what God has given me can never be taken from me, for His gifts are for all eternity.

The Gospel, the Higher Law

Jesus Christ brought the good news, the Gospel, that there was a higher law than the law of karma and that law transcends the law of karma. It is the law of grace, or forgiveness. It is the law that frees you from the law of cause and effect, the law of consequence. On this plane, you reap where you have not sown. The gifts of God are simply poured out upon us.

Power Without Direction

We know now, from a scientific standpoint, that death could be overcome by stamping the subconscious mind with the conviction of eternal youth and eternal life. The subconscious, being simply power without direction, carries out orders without questioning.

Christianity

Working under the direction of the superconscious, the Christ or God within you, the resurrection of the body would be accomplished. Humankind would no longer throw off the body in death. Christianity is founded upon the forgiveness of sins and an empty tomb.

Lighten Your Burden

I decree that Christ within is the light within me.

I affirm that all doubt and fear is consumed by His light.

Free to Be

I decree that God utilizes every person and every situation to bring me my heart's desires.

I affirm that hindrances are friendly and obstacles springboards. I now jump into my good.

Wind Yourself Up

When the almighty superconscious floods the subconscious with love, your whole life will changed. Resentment will hold you in a state of torment and imprisonment in your subconscious mind. You must wind yourself up with positive spoken words.

Manifestation of Good

I decree seeing my good in a golden glow of glory.

I affirm seeing my field shining white with the harvest.

See Clearly

It is impossible to see clearly while in the throes of the carnal mind. Doubts and fear poison the mind and body, and imagination runs riot, attracting disaster and disease. In steadily repeating the affirmation, "I cast this burden on the Christ within and go free," the vision clears, and with it a feeling of relief, and sooner or later comes the manifestation of good, be it health, happiness, or supply.

Casting and Seeing

Give thanks that you are saved, even though you seem surrounded by the enemy, the situation of lack or disease. How long must one remain in the dark? Until you can see in the dark, and casting the burden enables you to see in the dark.

Believe

I decree that God is my unfailing and immediate supply of all good.

I affirm that I am powerful and poised to receive.

Active Faith

To impress the subconscious, active faith is always essential. Faith without works is dead. Jesus Christ showed active faith when He commanded the multitude to sit down on the ground before He gave thanks for the loaves and the fishes. Active faith is the bridge over which you pass to your promised land.

With Music and Dancing

I decree that my greatest expectations
are realized in a miraculous way.

I affirm that I water my wilderness with faith
and suddenly it blossoms as the rose.

Rhythm

The subconscious is often impressed through music—a fourth dimensional quality that releases the soul from imprisonment. It makes wonderful things seem possible, and easy to accomplish. Perfect harmony and releases the imagination. Rhythm and harmony of music and motion carry forth freedom with tremendous power.

Make Believe

Continually making believe impresses the subconscious. If you make believe you are rich and successful, in due time you will reap.

Choose Whom You Serve

I decree that God's plans for me are built upon a solid rock, I shall not fear.

I affirm that fear and poverty have no place in my thought life—only the God of truth and freedom will I serve.

Misdirected Energy

There is no peace or happiness for you until you have erased all fear from the subconscious. Fear is misdirected energy and must be redirected or transmuted into faith.

God the Giver

The subconscious is impressed with the truth that God is the Giver and Gift. Therefore, as one is one with the Giver, you are one with the Gift. A splendid statement is, "I now thank God the Giver for God the Gift."

Fear or Faith

Humankind has so long separated ourselves from God's good and His supply through thoughts of separation and lack, that sometimes it takes dynamite to dislodge these false ideas from your subconscious, and the dynamite is a big situation. Watch yourself hourly to detect if your motive for action is fear or faith. Choose this day whom you shall serve, fear or faith.

No Defeat

I decree that nothing can defeat God.

I affirm, therefore, that nothing can defeat me.

Golden Links

Perhaps your fear is of someone's personality? If so, don't avoid the people feared. Be willing to meet them cheerfully, and they will either prove golden links in the chain of your good, or they will disappear harmoniously from your path.

Immune

Perhaps your fear is of disease or germs? You can only contract germs while vibrating at the same rate as the germ, and fear drags people down to the germ level. Of course, the disease-laden germ is the product of carnal mind, as all thought must objectify. Germs do not exist in the superconscious or divine mind.

The Twinkling of Your Eye

In the twinkling of an eye, your release will come when you realize there is no power in evil. The material world will fade away, and the fourth dimensional world, the world of the wondrous, will swing into manifestation.

Real Love

I decree that I wait patiently on the Lord.

I affirm that I trust in Him.

Pure Love

Pure, unselfish love draws to itself its own. It does not need to seek or demand. Scarcely anyone has the faintest conception of real love. Jealousy is the worst enemy of love, for the imagination runs riot, and invariably these fears objectify if they are not neutralized.

Divine Selection

When you send out real love, real love will return to you, either from this person or an equivalent, for if this person is not the divine selection, you will not want this individual. As you are one with God, you are one with the love that belongs to you by divine right.

Your Work

No one is a success in business unless they loves their work. The picture the artist paints for the love of art is the greatest work.

Fearless Faith

I decree that I now have the fearless
faith of the Christ within.

I affirm that at my approach, barriers
vanish and obstacles disappear.

Money Means...

No one can attract money if they despise it. Many people are kept in poverty by saying, "Money means nothing to me. I have a contempt for people who have it." This is the reason so many artists are poor. Their contempt for money separates them from it.

Supply Separation

An incorrect attitude of mind about money separates you from your supply. You must be in harmony with what you want to attract. Money is God in manifestation, as freedom from want and limitation; but it must be always kept in circulation and put to right uses.

Grim Vengeance

Hoarding and saving react with grim vengeance. This does not mean that you should not have houses and lots, stocks and bonds, for the barns of the righteous shall be full (see Psalm 144:13). It means you should not hoard even the principal if an occasion arises when money is necessary.

Let It Go

In letting money go out fearlessly and cheerfully, you open the way for more to come in, for God is your unfailing and inexhaustible supply. This is the spiritual attitude toward money.

No Hoarding Allowed

I decree that all fear is now banished in the name of Jesus Christ, for I know there is no power to hurt me.

I affirm that God is the One and only Power.

The Love of Money

Money in itself is good and beneficial, but used for destructive purposes, hoarded and saved, or considered more important than love, brings disease and disaster, and the loss of the money itself.

The Path of Love

Follow the path of love, and all things are added, for God is love, and God is supply. Follow the path of selfishness and greed, and the supply vanishes.

Violating the Law of Use

An old woman's arms gradually became paralyzed from holding on to things, and eventually she was considered incapable of looking after her affairs and her wealth was handed over to others to manage.

Violation of the Law of Love

In ignorance of the law, you bring about your own destruction. All disease, all unhappiness come from the violation of the law of love. Our boomerangs of hate, resentment, and criticism return to us laden with sickness and sorrow.

His Wonders to Perform

I decree that I am in perfect harmony with God, for He knows nothing of obstacles, time or space—only completion.

I affirm that God works in unexpected ways, His wonders to perform.

A Lost Art

Love seems almost a lost art, but the person with the knowledge of Spiritual Law knows it must be regained, for without it, we become as *"a noisy gong or a clanging cymbal"* (1 Corinthians 13:1).

Ditches Filled

I decree that my ditches are dug deep with faith and understanding and my heart's desire comes to pass in a surprising way.

I affirm that my ditches will be filled at the right time, bringing all that I have asked for and more.

In Thought

You are each other's keeper, in thought, and everyone should know that who you love dwells in the secret place of the Most High, and abides under the shadow of the Almighty. No evil will befall them there, neither shall any plague come near their home. Perfect love casts out fear. Whoever fears is not made perfect in love—love is the fulfilling of the law.

Ask and Receive

I decree and give thanks that I now receive
the righteous desires of my heart.

I affirm that mountains are removed, valleys
exalted and every crooked place made straight.

Demand the Lead

Speak the word and then do not do anything until you get a definite lead. Demand the lead, saying, "Infinite Spirit, reveal to me the way. Let me know if there's anything for me to do."

Quite Startling

Answers from the Infinite Spirit will come through intuition, or hunch, a chance remark from someone, or a passage in a book, etc. The answers are sometimes quite startling in their exactness.

Open the Way

Giving opens the way for receiving. To create activity in finances, we should give. Tithing, or giving one tenth of our income, is sure to bring increase. Many of the richest men in this country have been tithers and have never known it to fail as an investment.

The Tenth Part

The tenth part goes forth and returns blessed and multiplied—but the gift or tithe must be given with love and cheerfulness, for God loveth a cheerful giver (2 Corinthians 9:7).

The Fulfillment Kingdom

I decree that I'm in the Kingdom of fulfillment.

I affirm that I have perfect confidence in God and God has perfect confidence in me.

You the Master

Bills should be paid cheerfully. All money should be sent forth fearlessly and with a blessing. This attitude of mind makes you the master of your money. Your spoken word then opens vast reservoirs of wealth.

Hand in Hand

You limit your supply by limited vision. The vision and action must go hand in hand.

Easy and Possible

I decree that with God, all things are easy and possible now. I stand aside and watch God work.

I affirm how it interests me to see how quickly and easily He brings the desires of my heart to pass.

Points the Way

So often, we go for one thing and find another. Intuition is a spiritual faculty and does not explain but simply points the way.

Mysterious Leadings

You may receive a lead during a time of confusion. The idea that comes may seem quite irrelevant, but some of God's leadings are mysterious.

Put to Flight

I decree that I now put to flight the
army of negative thoughts.

I affirm that they feed on fear and starve on faith.

Congestion

I believe congestion of things causes congestion in the body. When you violate the law of use, your body is paying the penalty. So give thanks that divine order is established in your mind, body, and affairs.

Instantaneous Healing

A person might receive instantaneous healing through the realization of his or her body being a perfect idea in God's divine mind, and therefore whole and perfect. But if individuals continue their destructive thinking, hoarding, hating, fearing, condemning, the disease will return (see Matthew 12:43-45).

No Place

I decree that judgment and condemnation have no place in my thoughts, words, or actions.

I affirm that what I think, say, and do will attract similar responses from others.

Permanent Healing

Our soul, or subconscious mind, must be washed whiter than snow for permanent healing. Jesus Christ says, *"Judge not, and ye shall not be judged: condemn not, and ye shall not be condemned"* (Luke 6:37). Many people attract disease and unhappiness through judging and condemning judgment others. What you condemn in others, you attract to yourself!

Freedom

I decree that my good is a perfect and permanent idea in His divine mind and must manifest, for there is nothing to prevent.

I affirm and cast every burden on the Christ within and I go free.

Lost and Found

I decree that I can only lose what doesn't belong to me by divine right or isn't good enough for me.

I affirm that there is no loss God's divine mind. Therefore, I cannot lose anything that is rightfully mine.

No Loss

Infinite Intelligence is never too late. He knows the way of recovery. There is no loss in His divine mind. Therefore, I cannot lose anything that belongs to me. It will be restored or I will receive its equivalent.

No Debt

I decree that there is no debt in God's divine mind. No one owes me anything.

I affirm that all is squared—God sends forth love and forgiveness.

A Fearless Loving Heart

I decree that I am identified in love
with the Spirit of God.

I affirm that God protects my interests and His
divine idea now comes out of every situation.

I decree that the light of the Christ now streams
throughout my mind, body, and affairs.

I affirm clearly hearing the voice of glad
tidings of personal joy and success.

I decree that my heart is a perfect idea in God's divine
mind and is now in its right place, doing its right work.
It is a happy heart, a fearless heart and a loving heart.

I affirm that the light of the Christ streams
through my body and I give thanks for
my radiant health and happiness.

ABOUT

Florence Scovel Shinn

Florence Scovel Shinn (1871-1940) was born in Camden, New Jersey, and is best known for her book *The Game of Life and How to Play It,* published in 1925, which she self-published. She wrote several other books and was also an accomplished pencil drawing illustrator. Her artwork appeared in numerous magazines and books including *Harper's* and popular novels.

Florence Scovel Shinn attended the Pennsylvania Academy of the Fine Arts in Philadelphia. She and her husband moved to New York where he wrote three plays in which his wife played a leading role. Later in life, during the early 19th century, she became known as a "New Thought spiritual teacher," in the company of writers such as Mary Baker Eddy, Phineas Quimby, and Charles Fillmore.

THANK YOU FOR READING THIS BOOK!

If you found any of the information helpful, please take a few minutes and leave a review on the bookselling platform of your choice.

BONUS GIFT!

Don't forget to sign up to try our newsletter and grab your free personal development ebook here:

soundwisdom.com/classics